REFLECTIONS
ON THE
REVOLUTION
IN EGYPT

*Many of the writings associated with this
Working Group will be published by the Hoover Institution.
Materials published to date, or in production, are listed below.*

ESSAY SERIES:
THE GREAT UNRAVELING: THE REMAKING OF THE MIDDLE EAST

[For a list of books published under the auspices of the
WORKING GROUP ON ISLAMISM AND THE INTERNATIONAL ORDER,
please see page 76.]

HERBERT & JANE DWIGHT WORKING GROUP ON ISLAMISM AND THE INTERNATIONAL ORDER

ESSAY SERIES: THE GREAT UNRAVELING: THE REMAKING OF THE MIDDLE EAST

REFLECTIONS
ON THE
REVOLUTION
IN EGYPT

Samuel Tadros

HOOVER INSTITUTION PRESS
Stanford University   Stanford, California

www.hoover.org

Hoover Institution Press Publication No. 648

Hoover Institution at Leland Stanford Junior University, Stanford, California, 94305-6010

First printing 2014
21 20 19 18 17 16 15 14   9 8 7 6 5 4 3 2 1

Manufactured in the United States of America

The paper used in this publication meets the minimum requirements of the American National Standard for Information Sciences— Permanence of Paper for Printed Library Materials, ANSI/NISO Z39.48-1992. ♾

Cataloging-in-Publication Data is available from the Library of Congress.
ISBN 978-0-8179-1745-6 (pbk.: alk. paper)
ISBN 978-0-8179-1746-3 (epub)
ISBN 978-0-8179-1747-0 (mobi)
ISBN 978-0-8179-1748-7 (PDF)

*The Hoover Institution gratefully acknowledges
the following individuals and foundations
for their significant support of the*

HERBERT AND JANE DWIGHT WORKING GROUP
ON ISLAMISM AND THE INTERNATIONAL ORDER:

Herbert and Jane Dwight

Beall Family Foundation

Stephen Bechtel Foundation

Lynde and Harry Bradley Foundation

Mr. and Mrs. Clayton W. Frye Jr.

Lakeside Foundation

CONTENTS

The Great Unraveling:
The Remaking of the Middle East

IT'S A MANTRA, but it is also true: the Middle East is being unmade and remade. The autocracies that gave so many of these states the appearance of stability are gone, their dreaded rulers dispatched to prison or exile or cut down by young people who had yearned for the end of the despotisms. These autocracies were large prisons, and in 2011, a storm overtook that stagnant world. The spectacle wasn't pretty, but prison riots never are. In the Fertile Crescent, the work of the colonial cartographers—Gertrude Bell, Winston Churchill, and Georges Clemenceau—are in play as they have never been before. Arab nationalists were given to lamenting that they lived in nation-states "invented" by Western powers in the aftermath of the Great War. Now, a century later, with the ground burning in Lebanon, Syria, and Iraq and the religious sects at war, not even the most ardent nationalists can be sure that they can put in place anything better than the old order.

Men get used to the troubles they know, and the Greater Middle East seems fated for grief and breakdown. Outside powers approach it with dread; merciless political contenders have the run of it. There is swagger in Iran and a belief that the radical theocracy can bully its rivals into submission. There was a period when the United States provided a modicum of order in these Middle Eastern lands. But pleading fatigue, and financial scarcity at home, we have all but announced the end of that stewardship. We are poorer for that abdication, and the Middle East is thus left to the mercy of predators of every kind.

We asked a number of authors to give this spectacle of disorder their best try. We imposed no rules on them, as we were sure their essays would take us close to the sources of the malady.

FOUAD AJAMI
Senior Fellow, Hoover Institution—
Cochairman, Herbert and Jane Dwight Working Group
on Islamism and the International Order

CHARLES HILL
Distinguished Fellow of the Brady-Johnson Program
in Grand Strategy at Yale University;
Research Fellow, Hoover Institution—
Cochairman, Herbert and Jane Dwight Working Group
on Islamism and the International Order

Reflections on the Revolution in Egypt

SAMUEL TADROS

It is said that . . . [1]

It is said that . . . once upon a time / They stole our
    country, the Americans
They will enter Baghdad by noon / By evening they
    will enter Egypt

It is said that . . . that what? / Our people grabbed the
    light with their hands
It is said that . . . generation after generation / Egypt
    was born in Tahrir
It is said that . . . our dawn is arising / And Roses are
    blossoming in the street[2]

(AMIN HADDAD)

———

"But I cannot stand forward, and give praise or blame
to any thing which relates to human actions, and
human concerns, on a simple view of the object,
as it stands stripped of every relation, in all the
nakedness and solitude of metaphysical abstraction.
Circumstances (which with some gentlemen pass for
nothing) give in reality to every political principle its
distinguishing colour, and discriminating effect.
The circumstances are what render every civil and
political scheme beneficial or noxious to mankind."

(EDMUND BURKE: *Reflections on the Revolution in France*)

———

"It was not an event depending on chance or
contingency. It was inevitable; it was necessary;
it was planted in the nature of things."

(EDMUND BURKE: *Reflections on the Revolution in France*)

---

1. The poem was written by Amin Haddad ten days before the
fall of Baghdad in 2003 and sung by the band Eskenderella. The
poem reflects the feeling of helplessness and ends with a depress-
ing note.

2. After the Egyptian revolution, new lines were added to the
song, reflecting the newly discovered optimism and salvation found
in the square.

At 4:34 a.m. Cairo time on March 20, 2003, coalition forces led by the United States began their invasion of Iraq. Less than six hours later security lines in Cairo's Tahrir Square were being overrun by the most unlikely protesters: students of the American University in Cairo. Egyptian opposition parties had called for a protest at one o'clock in Tahrir, but three hours earlier 1,000 students had taken the initiative, surprised security forces, and managed to reach the square. The smell of euphoria was in the air as the students set their gaze on a building a few blocks from the square, that symbolized US hegemony over their country, the fortified US Embassy. The mass of people did not hesitate as they attacked line after line of security forces trying to break through, their attacks bearing fruit. They reached Omar Makram Mosque and then set foot on Simon Bolivar Square. "Tell Bush, tell Blair . . . Iraq is not Afghanistan," they shouted. There their attacks fell short; the security forces were better organized, and they could not break their lines no matter how much they tried. Some fell on the sides, their faces covered in blood; they were carried by their comrades. Half the protesters managed to reach the street leading to the Nile Corniche. Bringing traffic to a halt, they broke for freedom and tried to surround the British Embassy. They failed to encircle it, and two hours later they returned and joined their comrades in Simon Bolivar Square. They made a last attack and broke security lines back to Tahrir Square.

Opposition activists had arrived by then. Thousands were now in the square. They would attempt several times to reach the US Embassy but be rebuffed. Circles were forming in the square, graffiti was being drawn on the asphalt, and people were singing. Magda El-Roumi's famous song "The Street Is Ours" could be heard in the square. Voices chanting, "the street is ours . . . the square is ours . . . tomorrow Egypt will be ours." That generation of Egyptians had never seen anything like it. Egypt had not seen anything like this since the bread riots of 1977. The next day demonstrators started in Al-Azhar Mosque and took over the square again. Clashes continued throughout the day, and a fire truck used to disperse the crowds was reportedly set on fire. In the following days police arrested numerous activists of all political stripes. What remained of the crowd's spirit died twenty days later as they saw on TV Iraqis bring down Saddam Hussein's statue in Baghdad. The honor and dignity of a nation stretching from the Gulf to the Atlantic Ocean was lost in the streets of Baghdad.

The gods must have been rolling the dice that day on March 20, 2003. Little did the protesters in Tahrir Square know they were writing the first line in the story of the Egyptian revolution.

That Egypt's revolution has failed is hardly disputable today. The excitement of those magical eighteen days in Tahrir Square and the hopes of a dawn of democracy in Egypt are long gone. Replacing them is widespread despair among Egypt's revolutionary activists and their international cheerleaders, and who would blame them? The man they sought to topple enjoys his freedom after two years in prison, the old faces of his regime are now back, and the revolutionary activists—those who are not cheering the very military they were chanting against two years earlier—are now among the jailed, the cursed, the emigrant, and the depressed.

It is true some still believe the revolution continues or, more fancifully, the ouster of Mohamed Morsi is but the second wave of the original revolution. Joining the ranks of the delusional is the American Secretary of State John Kerry, who suggested the revolution was "stolen" by the Muslim Brotherhood, with Egypt now apparently set on the right path to democracy. But outside of those few voices—and regardless of whether one believes that Egypt is witnessing a counterrevolution, as the author contends, or a coup, or that no revolution occurred in the first place, as

Hugh Roberts[3] argues in the pages of the *London Review of Books*—the general consensus is that Egypt has returned to an authoritarian grip albeit this time with the masses cheering along. Whatever happened on January 25 failed miserably in transforming the country in the direction of a true democracy.

For those lamenting the failure of a revolution that captivated the world, the blame is usually placed on two forces: Egypt's military and the Muslim Brotherhood. A military that never accepted the notion of civilian control and that aimed to protect its exclusive domination of the state and its economy and a Brotherhood that ruled in a noninclusive manner and alienated many segments of Egypt's population have formed the basis of the explanations given by analysts as to why Egypt reached the state it is in today.

Remarkably little attention has been given to the actions and choices of Egypt's non-Islamist

---

3. Hugh Roberts, "The Revolution That Wasn't," *London Review of Books,* Volume 35, No. 17, September 12, 2013.

revolutionaries. Besides the usual criticism of their organizational weakness and the more recent critical look at those among them who supported the military coup, they have largely escaped any critical examination and hence blame. This is all the more surprising given the fact that three years earlier, when the crowds occupied Tahrir Square, both the media and Western analysts fixed their gazes on those young men and women, often described as liberals, democrats, moderates, and secular, to the extent of seeing nothing but them. Egypt's revolutionaries were hailed as the heroic force that ended what seemed like an eternal dichotomy between repressive authoritarian regimes and totalitarian Islamists. People like Google executive Wael Ghonim, April 6 founder Ahmed Maher, and international diplomat Mohamed ElBaradei would create the much-awaited third alternative or route.

On January 25, 2011, thousands of Egyptians—some of them veterans of earlier demonstrations against Hosni Mubarak, some of them demonstrating for the first time in their lives—took to the streets to demand change. Three days later hundreds of thousands joined them, and fifteen days later Mubarak resigned as Egypt's president. Who were those revolutionaries and where did they come from? What was their composition ideologically and organizationally? Why were they angry with the Mubarak regime and decided to bring it down? What were their demands and aspirations for a new Egypt? And how did they go about attempting to achieve them? To understand the story of Egypt's revolution, one has to begin, not on January 25, 2011, but years earlier when those revolutionaries were meeting one another for the first time and acquiring the skills that they would later use to bring down the regime.

The lack of a thorough investigation of Egypt's revolutionaries creates a serious gap in our understanding of the events that unfolded in the past three years. From their decision to call for mass demonstrations on January 25, 2011, their rejection of participating in politics, their calls for an end to the Supreme Council of the Armed Forces (SCAF) rule, their continuous demonstrations and violent clashes with the police, and the choices they made in the parliamentary and presidential elections, Egypt's revolutionaries were not helpless victims but actors who affected and shaped the direction of the country. As Egypt continues on its destructive path into the abyss, it is important to examine what role the revolutionaries played in its trajectory.

On December 12, 2004, the Egyptian Movement for Change held its first demonstration. The movement quickly became known by its slogan *Kefaya* (Enough). Kefaya demonstrators were few in numbers, but their public act of defiance created a stir in the dull political scene that was Mubarak's Egypt. The demonstrators' chants, while attacking the regime's foreign policy and its capitulation to US and Israeli hegemony, also targeted the regime's domestic policies and, more importantly, the regime itself. Mubarak; his wife, Suzanne; and their son Gamal, rumored to be groomed for the throne, were no longer off-limits. A red line seemed to have been crossed. Taboos were being shattered.

The movement had its roots in the pro-Palestinian demonstrations in October 2000, with the start of the second intifada, but those had quickly fizzled away. Smaller campaigns had followed calling for the boycott of American products and organizing aid convoys to the Palestinians, but they had little effect. The American invasion of Iraq in 2003 created the first real spark that gathered those opposition activists together. In July 2004 a new Egyptian government was sworn in that included a significant number of new faces, businessmen who had prospered in the private sector were recruited for government ministries. With Mubarak's health rumored to be in decline and Gamal's increasing public role, a transition moment seemed to be in the air. Roughly 300 intellectuals and activists gathered to write and sign Kefaya's manifesto during the hot summer months. Their demands were hardly small. They demanded real political change in the country. Mubarak's fourth term was to end in September 2005, and they wanted it to be his last. Gamal shall not inherit us from his father, they insisted.

Who were the 300 men who signed Kefaya's manifesto? They came from all stripes of the Egyptian opposition. Nearly all of them were veterans of the roaring '70s. George Ishak was the movement's first coordinator. A communist, he had used his official position in the administration of Catholic schools in Egypt to gather a group of young men around him. Abdel Halim Kandil was a committed Nasserite who was editor in chief of the leading Nasserite newspaper, in which he cursed Mubarak for abandoning Nasser's domestic project and his anti-American foreign policy. Abdel Wahab El Misiri, who was later chosen to lead the movement, dedicated his life to writing about Jews and Israel. His conspiracy-driven mind led him to believe the Camp David accords included secret clauses calling for the banning of his writings. Kamal Khalil was a Revolutionary Socialist, the name given to Egypt's Trotskyites, and a veteran demonstrator. Magdy Ahmed Hussein was the son of Ahmed Hussein, Egypt's fascist leader in the '30s and '40s. In the '80s Magdy had made the political transformation from socialism to Islamism, with the final outcome uniting the worst of both worlds. Kamal Abu Eita was another Nasserite who had never missed an anti-regime demonstration in his life.

None of these men could excite a revolutionary populace, let alone one that had been apathetic for years. They were more representative of the ills of Egypt than its cure. Formed by a group of communists, Islamists, and Nasserites, there was nothing novel about its message with the exception of its bald animosity toward Mubarak and his son. The message was simply the repetition of every long-held myth and demand of the Egyptian opposition; these men decried social and economic exploitation, believing that the country was rich but was being stolen by corrupt businessmen and that the regime was serving American and Israeli interests. Their hatred of Mubarak dwarfed the hatred they expressed toward the United States and Israel, and anti-Semitism was rampant among them. "Their real objection to Mubarak was not his authoritarianism, but his abandonment, like that of Sadat before him, of the pan-Arab vision Nasser had proclaimed," Roberts said.[4] As Abdel Halim Kandil stated: "Egypt falls under American

---

4. Hugh Roberts, "The Revolution That Wasn't," *London Review of Books,* Volume 35, No. 17, September 12, 2013.

hegemony and Israeli occupation, and the regime is loyal to them. Therefore, opposition toward Israel and America is a cornerstone of Kefaya's program."[5] What was novel was their decision to bring their message out of the salons of the leftist intellectuals and to the street.

Kefaya activists were soon creating sister organizations, the most important of which was Youth for Change. The initial members were hardly surprising. They were the sons and daughters of veteran leftist activists. However, they had at their disposal a tool not available to their parents' generation: blogging. Blogs became very powerful tools not just for self-expression, but more importantly for disseminating information. Through videos of police torture, election fraud, or demonstrations, activists were reaching a new generation of young, middle-class Egyptians. Citizen journalism was the new hit in town as thousands of young Egyptians started blogs. Naturally journalistic standards were hardly present and the quality and truthfulness of many of them were

---

5. Tarek Masoud, "US must back democracy in Egypt regardless," *Los Angeles Times*, February 9, 2011.

lacking. But with state propaganda techniques unchanged for decades, the activists held a significant advantage in the war of perception. Blogs also served as an important forum for networking. A bond was being created between activists across the political spectrum.

Blogs were hardly the domain of leftist activists alone. Numerous young Muslim Brotherhood members began blogging, and the new phenomenon caught the attention of analysts desperate for a "moderate Brotherhood." Kefaya was not the only group that took notice of the winds of change unleashed by President George W. Bush's Freedom Agenda and the opportunities it presented. The Muslim Brotherhood took note and attempted to present a new face. It increasingly coordinated with the rest of the opposition, though unlike them it always remained aware of the red lines imposed by the regime. Women were being presented as candidates for Parliament, and a platform for change was presented to the public and more importantly to Western analysts and policy-makers.

Egypt's official opposition parties were also influenced by the changing political environment.

The parliamentary elections of 2005 were extremely frustrating to the two main parties: *Al Wafd* and *El Tagamuu*. Many of their members, especially the younger ones, had already begun to question the wisdom of their parties' tamed opposition approach to the regime. The man who best embodied those changes was Ayman Nour. An unimpressive journalist with Al Wafd newspaper, Nour had distinguished himself with fabricated and sensationalist stories. His relationship with the regime was hardly bad. He twice won a seat in Egypt's Parliament and had been useful as a controlled opposition face to use as a mouthpiece when the regime faced an international scandal over its police behavior in the El Kosheh massacre of Copts. His ambitions were matched only by his ego. He left Al Wafd in 2001 and sought to establish his own party. When he received the party approval from the regime-controlled committee in October 2004, it was another sign of the regime's approval. Suddenly on January 30, 2005, Nour was arrested on charges of forging applications for his new party. While the charges were correct, leveling them was indisputably a political decision.

Nour's real crime was perceived to be his meeting with former Secretary of State Madeleine Albright in which he presented himself as a liberal alternative to the regime. His liberalism, of course, had very little to do with the actual meaning of the term: but he wasn't an Islamist, and for many that automatically made him a liberal. More importantly, between October and January, the Orange Revolution had taken place in Ukraine and the regime became scared. Nour was allowed to stand against Mubarak in the presidential election in September of that year, but his fate was sealed. He soon landed in jail, though not before his case had become a cause célèbre for Western journalists, analysts, and governments.

Kefaya's last serious stand was in the spring of 2006 when it supported two judges who were investigated by the regime for their protests against election fraud during the parliamentary elections. The Judges Club had been fighting for judicial independence for years and had increasingly played a vocal role in criticizing regime practices. The regime viewed a challenge by the judiciary as a serious threat and moved swiftly to silence the judges and attack protesters in solidarity with them.

Kefaya's efforts did not bear fruit, and the movement soon lost steam. With its largest demonstration attracting no more than a few thousand participants, the movement was hardly a challenge to the regime. Nevertheless, while it lasted, it served an important role in linking Egypt's leftist, Islamist, Nasserite, and quasi-liberal opposition. More profoundly it served as a training ground for many of the young stars who would later play a key role in the Egyptian revolution.

"Congratulations on the Fall of Saddam's Statue. . . .
May the rest of the Statues Fall"

> (A letter published in the Nasserite newspaper
> *Al-Arabi Al-Nassery* in April 2003)

"So it is the policy of the United States to seek and
support the growth of democratic movements and
institutions in every nation and culture, with the
ultimate goal of ending tyranny in our world."

(PRESIDENT GEORGE W. BUSH, second Inaugural Address)

THE FALL OF BAGHDAD IN 2003 sent shock waves
throughout the Arab world. Saddam's promises of
defiance and resistance and his cartoonish Information Minister Mohammed Saeed al-Sahhaf's
press conferences had led many Arabs to believe
that Iraq would not fall easily to the invading
forces. On April 9, reality finally hit home. The
humiliation that was felt in the Arab street was
reminiscent of the 1967 defeat. The total moral,
political, and civilizational bankruptcy of Arab
regimes was laid bare.

Arab regimes, while hardly weeping for the
demise of Saddam, were put on notice. Signs
were abounding since the 9/11 attacks that
the US was no longer content with the regional

order. The region's endemic diseases were no longer a local matter but had hit the shores of America. The US was searching for answers and solutions. The regional order Pax Americana had established and maintained had proven not only unsustainable but also deeply flowed. Washington was full of talk of the region's democracy deficit and its role in fomenting extremism, and US policy in the region looked poised for a major shift. Few missed the tone of Bush's second Inaugural Address and its promises of promoting democracy. The message was echoed two weeks later in his State of the Union address. The clearest statement was, however, delivered in Cairo by Secretary of State Condoleezza Rice: "For 60 years, my country, the United States, pursued stability at the expense of democracy in this region here in the Middle East—and we achieved neither. Now, we are taking a different course."

The ramifications of the US policy shift were immediately felt throughout the region. Behind closed doors Arab regimes were being pressured to open up and allow genuine opposition. After ridiculing calls for constitutional changes, Mubarak suddenly reversed course and in February 2005 announced his intention to allow a multicandidate presidential election for the first time. The pressure excreted on the Egyptian regime was forcing it to remove part of its own pressure on the opposition. While the regime's policies hardly allowed free competition, the vulnerability of Mubarak's regime was being exposed to its citizens and to the opposition, which recognized a golden opportunity to obtain more concessions.

But the most important legacy of President Bush's Freedom Agenda was not the pressure it put on regimes, for that soon subsided, but the new world that was opened to dissidents and opponents of Mubarak. Dissidents were suddenly international celebrities, and the newly acquired attention protected many of them from the worst of the regime's practices. Egyptian activists and bloggers were showered with invitations to meetings and speeches in the US and Europe, and the regime was put more on the defensive as its practices received further scrutiny and criticism. More consequential, however, were the tools and opportunities that were suddenly put at the dissidents' disposal.

In December 2002 Secretary of State Colin Powell had announced the creation of the Middle East Partnership Initiative (MEPI). One of its aims, he indicated, was "to close the freedom gap with projects to strengthen civil society, expand political participation, and lift the voices of women." Together with MEPI, the US Agency for International Development began to focus more on democracy funding in the region. US democracy promotion organizations such as the National Endowment for Democracy, the International Republican Institute, the National Democratic Institute, and Freedom House received more funding to bridge that freedom gap.

The results were nothing less than spectacular. Thousands of Egyptians traveled to the United States in a variety of programs that aimed to provide them with the necessary tools to change their societies. Thousands of training sessions were held in the US, the region, and around the world to teach activists new ways to organize and mobilize. They learned how to use new technology to their advantage. Hundreds of Egyptian civil society organizations received funding for political training and election monitoring. Experiences were being transferred as veterans from pro-democracy movements in Eastern Europe trained Egyptian activists on how to challenge the authoritarian regime. Regional ties were being created as thousands of activists from across the Arab world were being introduced to one another and sharing their experiences.

Nevertheless in the rush to support activists and dissidents and close the freedom gap, something was largely missing: the content that would fill the gap. Action, not theory, was what was sought. Activists were being provided tools but no substance to use them for. Human rights activists were being trained on how to document abuses, but no one paid attention to explaining the intellectual foundation of why these were considered abuses in the first place. Newer computers were being provided to Egyptian newspapers, but the same anti-American, anti-Semitic, conspiracy theory-driven articles were being written. Some of the programs, like those run by any bureaucracy, and the American one is no exception, suffered from the problem of giving people a fish per day instead of training them how to fish. More profoundly, no one paid the slightest attention to explaining why fishing was good in the first place. In a region that had not developed a natural rights discourse, democracy assistance only exasperated its ills instead of helping cure them. Human freedom was being downgraded and replaced by a mere tool; democracy and democracy promotion became a goal in itself with no understanding of what that democracy might produce.

Activists were being trained, but who were they and what did they advocate? No one seemed to care. Anyone who was neither part of the regime nor a member of a terrorist organization seemed to qualify for US benevolence. It mattered little if those activists were actively attempting to replace the oppressive regime with worse ones of the Islamist, Nasserite, or communist variant. Any regime opponent was described as a liberal and every beardless activist depicted a secular. While Western policy-makers spoke of a war of ideas being waged for the hearts and minds of the region's citizens, they hardly provided any ideas to compete with the prevalent leftist and Islamist ideas that dominated Arab culture. Ultimately they were only providing the existing anti-American ideologists with better tools.

With abundant funding, civil society organizations were becoming more attractive to young Egyptians than political parties. Some were genuine believers, but in a political environment in which opposition parties suffered from the same diseases afflicting the ruling one, civil society organizations provided a much-needed breathing space. They also provided an opportunity for personal development, fame, and economic advancement. But it was not any associations that were being promoted, but a particular kind—human rights NGOs. Funding was available for monitoring elections, documenting abuses, even video journalism, but not much more. A new generation of activists was trained to approach Egypt's democratic deficit from a rights perspective, not politics. People were trained how to protest and challenge autocracy; no one was trained on how to politically organize, formulate programs, and compromise. The depletion of talent from political parties would be a problem that would have a profound effect on the future of the Egyptian revolution.

~

We are sleeping on a volcano. . . . A wind of
revolution blows, the storm is on the horizon.

(ALEXIS DE TOCQUEVILLE)

BY 2008, AS KEFAYA HAD LOST whatever steam it
had, young activists were searching for alterna-
tives to challenge the regime. Egypt was witnessing a wave of labor strikes because of the
impact of the regime's privatization and neo-
liberal economic policies as well as to increased
leftist agitation especially by Revolutionary
Socialists. Textile workers in El Mahalla El Kubra
decided to hold a strike on April 6, 2008, until
their wage demands were met. The call for sup-
porting them was initiated by the Islamist Labor
Party and its leader Magdy Ahmed Hussein, but
the real action began when his call was adopted
by a group of young activists on Facebook. Later
known as the April 6 movement, the men and
women behind the Facebook group had their
roots in various anti-Mubarak groups such
as Kefaya, Ayman Nour's *Al Ghad* Party, and
the Labor Party. Overnight Egyptian Facebook
users were joining the group in droves. The
media started covering the phenomenon, and

the regime panicked. Labor strikes, the regime understood and could handle, but the prospect of middle-class youth joining in was novel. Arrests were made to try to dampen their spirit. No one knew what to expect. Would people joining a Facebook group online actually show up and protest? Learning from the experience of other international protest movements, April 6 began suggesting innovative ways in which people could participate (e.g., wearing black T-shirts, not buying anything that day).

April 6 claimed success as the streets of Cairo were less crowded than usual that day. In reality, people were not actually taking part in a strike as much as they were genuinely afraid of what might happen because of the intense media hype. The strike's most important event took place in the city of El Mahalla, where textile workers clashed violently with the police and, in a scene that would become iconic for activists, brought down Mubarak's huge picture and stepped on it with their feet. Important lessons were being learned by activists. Social media was a powerful tool. Although the thousands of people who clicked their support for a Facebook group did not show up and protest, it still frightened the regime. Nonideological calls for protest that appealed to abstract principles and values had a higher potential of gathering a diverse group of people. Street mobilization was the way to threaten the regime and not political organization. The prospect of urban middle-class youth joining the anti-Mubarak protests could be the spark everyone was searching for.

Later actions by April 6 were less successful. Calls for protests on Mubarak's birthday or the April 6 anniversary were a resounding failure, but the movement did not disappear. Members continued to receive training on nonviolence from American and European organizations working on democracy promotion in the region. While Kefaya had attempted to build a consensus among its ideologically diverse communist, Nasserite, and Islamist members, April 6 needed to exert no such effort. The movement was completely devoid of ideas and ideologies. Its members shared a general leftist/Islamist tendency and hated Israel, the US, and Mubarak, but none of them could be mistaken for an ideologue or a deep thinker.

As 2009 was coming to a close, the sense of frustration among activists and an increasing number of upper-middle-class Egyptians was growing. American pressure on the regime to open up had weakened during Bush's last years in office and completely fizzled out under President Barack Obama, making the regime more comfortable cracking down on its opponents. Mubarak's fifth term in office was due to end in September 2011, and rumors of his deteriorating health were intensifying with his trip to Germany in March 2010 for medical treatment. His grandson's death in May 2009 was reported to have broken the man completely. With no declared successor, Cairo's rumor mill saw Gamal Mubarak's ascendency to the presidency as all but announced. With previous opposition fronts and movements failing to produce tangible results, activists were looking for an alternative and a savior. In their desperation they stumbled across the great liberal nope,[6] Mohamed ElBaradei.

------

6. David Schenker and Eric Trager, "Egypt's Great Liberal Nope," *The Weekly Standard,* January 23, 2012.

No man could be a more unlikely Godot for a country waiting in the train station than ElBaradei. A mediocre international bureaucrat whose claim to fame had more to do with European elites' dislike of President Bush than of any actual achievements of his own, he became the ideal candidate to stir Egypt's stagnant waters. The man's connection and knowledge of the country he aimed to lead was nonexistent, but that was hardly a drawback for Egypt's opposition. With ElBaradei an empty vessel with no political history but with an image of a statesman, people could project upon him their own views and imagine him to be anything they dreamed. Moreover, his lack of knowledge of the country and its politics meant that he needed guidance, and many a member of Egypt's opposition was happy to play the role of intermediary and controller. His international fame was an asset as the Mubarak regime could not treat him in the same manner that it dealt with the rest of the opposition.

The call for ElBaradei's nomination for Egypt's presidency was initiated on Facebook by a group of veteran activists. Thousands supported the call, and anticipation mounted as the date of his announced return to Egypt approached. On February 19, 2010, he finally landed. It was hardly Ruhollah Khomeini's triumphant return or that of Juan Peron. Less than a thousand gathered to greet him at the airport, but the mass hysteria only grew. Around him gathered the full spectrum of Egypt's opposition. The Muslim Brotherhood sent representatives, though the organization was cautious in not getting dragged into the muddle. They formed the National Association for Change. ElBaradei was its nominal head, though he hardly spent much time in the country after his "return." Conspiracy theorist Hassan Nafaa was the coordinator and Nasserite Hamdi Kandil the spokesperson. Echoing the national struggle for independence initiated by Saad Zaghloul in 1919, the group sought to receive a mandate from the people by getting them to sign its seven-point demands for political change. In the following months 130,000 signed the document. The number was significant, larger than anything the opposition had managed to gather in the past years, and highlighted the problem the regime was facing with upper-middle-class youth, but it was hardly a game changer. The Muslim Brotherhood's order to its followers to sign the document added an additional 800,000 signatures and clarified to any careful observer who actually had the machine and support necessary to rattle the status quo.

On June 6, 2010, a young man named Khaled Said was killed by two police detectives who arrested him in a cybercafé in Alexandria. Postmortem photographs of his corpse immediately went viral, shocking a nation. While there would be attempts later to mythologize Said by making him a political activist who exposed corruption, the power of his death was actually due to how ordinary he was. He was just another frustrated young man with no political leanings who dreamed of leaving Egypt. People could relate to him. They could have been him.

One person moved by Said's story was Google executive Wael Ghonim. He started a Facebook group called "We are all Khaled Said." Hundreds of thousands joined the group, which quickly became the center of efforts to change the country. Behind the scenes, Ghonim was coordinating with veterans of Egypt's protest movements such as April 6 who had a better knowledge of the country's political landscape and better techniques to bring about change. Campaigns were initiated calling on people to wear black on certain days and sit silently on main streets; and they began to find an echo on the streets. Said's death had finally tipped the balance in the minds of thousands of Egypt's upper-middle-class and middle-class youth. They were still not sure what could be done, but they were now willing to throw their lot behind any effort to change their country.

As the final months of 2010 were coming to a close, parliamentary elections were held. The National Association for Change called on political parties to boycott the elections. Hardly anyone obliged with the main opposition parties and the Muslim Brotherhood running candidates. Only after the first round of voting witnessed unprecedented irregularities did they oblige and withdraw from the second round. Even tame opposition parties like Al Wafd were frustrated. Hundreds of thousands of upper-middle-class and middle-class Egyptians saw

~

videos of ballot stuffing. Previously apolitical Facebook users were now angrily sharing those videos. Dark clouds were amassing in the skies of Cairo. People waited for the rain.

~

Hey O Square[7]

Hey O Square / Where have you been for a long time?
The sound of freedom united us / Finally our lives
    have a meaning
There is no turning back, our voice is heard /
    The dream finally is not prohibited
You broke the wall, lit the light / Gathered around
    you a broken people
We were born again / And the stubborn dream
    was born

"Bliss was it in that dawn to be alive,
But to be young was very Heaven!"

(WILLIAM WORDSWORTH: *The Prelude*)

------

7. Written after the revolution, it was sung by Cairokee and Aida El-Ayoubi.

Do you hear the people sing?[8]

Do you hear the people sing?
Singing the song of angry men?
It is the music of the people
Who will not be slaves again!
When the beating of your heart
Echoes the beating of the drums
There is a life about to start
When tomorrow comes!

FEW EGYPTIANS were keeping an eye on events in Tunisia after Mohamed Bouazizi's self-immolation. Tunisia, and the whole Arab Maghreb, had always been too remote from the collective consciousness of Egyptians. Modern Egypt's gaze had been set northward toward Europe or eastward toward the Arab Mashriq. However, when Tunisian President Zine el-Abidine Ben Ali addressed his nation on January 13, Egyptians began watching with interest; when he fled the country the next day, they were electrified. That day, the administrator of the "We are all Khaled Said" Facebook

---

8. Herbert Kretzmer, lyricist, "Do You Hear the People Sing?," *Les Misérables.*.

group, Wael Ghonim, made the first call for a revolution on January 25. Sixty years earlier on that date, the Egyptian police had battled British occupation forces and the day came to be known as National Police Day. A lot of water had passed under the bridges of the Nile in the intervening years, and the police had become the most hated symbol of the regime. Thousands clicked on Facebook indicating they were participating. Even veteran activists were not sure what to expect.

As the day progressed, thousands of protesters poured into Tahrir Square. They had marched through various districts of Cairo and attracted, for the first time, many apolitical citizens. Rumors were abounding. The Tunisian revolution has been a romantic fairy tale: it was short, with few deaths, the military siding with the people, and the dictator quickly fleeing the country. Egyptians began dreaming of a similar fairy tale. With a few thousand in Tahrir, an opposition leader was already talking about the crowd growing to a hundred thousand. According to shared stories on Facebook, Gamal Mubarak had already fled the country. The police attempted to control the crowd but was not excessively violent. As the day drew to a close, the police moved in and cleared the crowd in ten minutes.

In reality, Gamal had not fled and the regime had not fallen, but something equally important had happened: the barrier of fear had been shattered. With stories of protesters in the streets, real or imagined, the final obstacle to collective action had been overcome. Full-time activists and protesters were joined in droves by middle-class youth. Years of exclusion, a poor education system that prepared no one for future jobs, and high youth unemployment had finally come to haunt the regime. For decades the dream of those young men had been to leave the country and emigrate—temporarily to the Gulf or permanently to the West. Now they were taking their revenge. It is true the regime in its last years had accomplished an unprecedented growth rate and the country's economy was flourishing, but as Alexis de Tocqueville argued, "It is almost never when a state of things is the most detestable that it is smashed, but when, beginning to improve, it permits men to breathe, to reflect, to communicate their thoughts with each other, and to gauge by what they already have the extent of their rights and their grievances. The weight, although less heavy, seems then all the more unbearable."[9] Even those who were willing years earlier to give Gamal the benefit of the doubt were now in open revolt. The 2010 elections had left little doubt about the regime's lack of interest in real reform, and the myth of the possibility and durability of economic reform without political reform was finally being exposed as empty.

What were the demands of those who ignited the Egyptian revolution? Why were they angry at the Mubarak regime and, more importantly, what did they want to replace it with? More than two centuries ago, in his magnum opus, *Reflections on the Revolution in France,* Edmund Burke had warned, "The effect of liberty to individuals is that they may do what they please; we ought to see what it will please them to do, before we risk congratulations which may be soon turned into complaints."[10]

---

9. Alexis de Tocqueville, letter to Pierre Freslon, September 23, 1853.

10. Edmund Burke, *Reflections on the Revolution in France.*

Two chants would echo in the streets of Cairo and Tahrir Square during the magical eighteen days that followed: "The people want to bring down the regime" and "Bread, freedom, social justice." The two chants captured the nature of the Egyptian revolution and those who instigated it best. The crowd was united in its hatred of Mubarak for obvious reasons. The man had never excited the country he came to rule unexpectedly on an eventful day in 1981. A country accustomed to grandiosity and giants that in reality had brought it more misery than glory never warmed to a dwarf, and whatever tolerance it had for his mediocre rule had evaporated over the years. The second chant deserves more scrutiny.

A chant is naturally not expected to offer a program. It is merely a slogan or an aspiration; but in the case of the Egyptian revolution, it represented all the content there was. It is perhaps astonishing that in a country with one of the lowest prices of bread in the world, people would be demanding bread—yet that is what they did. In a country where people were accustomed to the state providing for their every need, the economic liberalization program that Gamal Mubarak had championed was viewed as an assault on the natural rights of Egyptians to the nanny state. What made it all the worse is that this assault was never articulated, explained, or defended. The Egyptian regime was happily feeding its people the same socialist slogans it had inherited from Gamal Abdel Nasser while at the same time, step by step, withdrawing from that socialist role. With the absence of a liberal discourse, socialist ideas and slogans dominated the public square, often interwoven with Islamist ones.

In this sense the Egyptian revolution is perhaps the most remarkable of revolutions. Its initiators sought to bring down Mubarak's regime in order to replace it with one that interfered more in their lives and limited their economic freedoms. The state had betrayed the Nasserite contract and taken the side of "corrupt businessmen." State intervention was not what was being detested, but what was being desired. As Hugh Roberts suggested: "A movement that wants those desiderata provided by government and, at the same time, wants the government to clear off has a coherence problem."[11] While often described as liberal, moderate, democratic, and secular, the groups that led the Egyptian revolution were neither liberal nor moderate. And for some, their secularism is of a questionable nature; and for most, their democratic credentials remain to be seen.

Two remaining myths of the Egyptian revolution are worth some reflection. It was fashionable then and is still remarkably fashionable now to claim that the revolution was peaceful. Such a description is devoid of the truth. The revolution could not have succeeded had the security forces not been broken, and that breaking was accomplished with great violence. More than a hundred police stations were ransacked and burned starting on January 28. Most of Egypt's prisons were attacked and 23,000 prisoners, both political and criminal, were freed. Massive looting targeted symbols of the regime such as the ruling party's headquarters as well as private property. Naturally, the security vacuum was an

---

11. Hugh Roberts, "The Revolution That Wasn't," *London Review of Books,* Volume 35, No. 17, September 12, 2013.

opportunity for many to take revenge as well as steal.

The Muslim Brotherhood's vital role in the revolution has been ignored, often intentionally, by other activists and their Western cheerleaders. Watching the narrative broadcast on TV during the revolution, one was tempted to believe there were no Islamists in Egypt. Although the Muslim Brotherhood was initially hesitant to join what seemed before January 25 as a risky adventure, at the critical moment on January 28 it provided its full support and with it its masses. Mosques as launching points for demonstrations were an ideal setting for the Brotherhood. Its members played a crucial role in fighting the police and defending protesters from attacks on the square. By the end of the revolution's eighteen days, the Brotherhood was the only political movement in the country that could claim some of its members as martyrs. No other revolutionary movement had that distinction besides football ultras.

"A desire for independence of this kind, stemming as it does from a specific, removable cause—the evil practices of a despotic government—is bound to be short-lived. Once the circumstances giving rise to it have passed away, it languishes and what at first sight seemed a genuine love of liberty proves to have been merely hatred of a tyrant."

(ALEXIS DE TOCQUEVILLE: *The Old Regime and the French Revolution*)

Stand Your Ground[12]

You are calling for dignity and they are replying
    with humiliation
Fear is afraid from you and your conscience has never
    betrayed you
You are the light of dawn and your chant is louder
    than the sound of bullets and betrayal
You have a God whose name is Right, justice and
    benevolence
No matter if a soul dies, the idea will not die

"Suppose that a great commotion arises in the street about something, let us say a lamp-post, which many influential persons desire to pull down. A grey-clad monk, who is the spirit of the Middle Ages, is approached upon the matter, and begins to say, in the arid manner of the Schoolmen, "Let us first of all consider, my brethren, the value of Light. If Light be in itself good—" At this point he is somewhat

---

12. A song by the band Cairokee.

43

excusably knocked down. All the people make a rush for the lamp-post, the lamp-post is down in ten minutes, and they go about congratulating each other on their unmediaeval practicality. But as things go on they do not work out so easily. Some people have pulled the lamp-post down because they wanted the electric light; some because they wanted old iron; some because they wanted darkness, because their deeds were evil. Some thought it not enough of a lamp-post, some too much; some acted because they wanted to smash municipal machinery; some because they wanted to smash something. And there is war in the night, no man knowing whom he strikes. So, gradually and inevitably, to-day, to-morrow, or the next day, there comes back the conviction that the monk was right after all, and that all depends on what is the philosophy of Light. Only what we might have discussed under the gas-lamp, we now must discuss in the dark."

(G. K. Chesterton: *Heretics*)

The feeling of jubilation in Tahrir Square on February 11 as Omar Suleiman read Mubarak's resignation was indescribable. That night, hardly anyone slept as hundreds of thousands celebrated in the streets. The next day, they woke up to a question: what happens next?

In reality, no one knew. No one had ever given that question much thought let alone prepared

44

for that day. The people had united in their demand for Mubarak to step down; what comes after was anyone's guess. The accidental coalition that had led to the fall of Mubarak was bound to collapse. The core of the conflict centered on the question of who had achieved that task: was it the army with its decision to side with the people, the Muslim Brotherhood for providing the troops necessary to turn a demonstration into a revolution, the ordinary men and women who suddenly rose after having been apathetic for decades, or the core of the revolutionaries—those who had struggled for years against the regime and then demolished the first brick in the regime's wall of oppression? Victory, as President John F. Kennedy pronounced, had a thousand fathers. The question could not be settled. Each had reason to mythologize his role. Each had reason to claim ownership. The claim of ownership of the revolution was not an abstract question, and it would have profound ramifications. Ownership meant entitlement, entitlement to set the future course of the country, maybe even entitlement to rule.

No group faced a harder dilemma over the question of the future than the revolutionaries. Young and old alike, veteran activists had devoted their lives to the fight against Mubarak. Now that the object of their hatred was gone, what were they to do with their lives? The eighteen magical days in Tahrir were not only the culmination of years of struggle but also their most glorious moment. The world was captivated by their struggle, journalists were flocking to interview them, and their faces were on the cover of magazines. Even a Nobel Peace Prize did not seem far-fetched at that moment. Who could blame them if they remained attached to the square? Capturing the spirit of the time, the band Eskenderella added new lines to its famous song; "Egypt was born in Tahrir," it proclaimed. In reality it hadn't, but many of the revolutionaries had. There was life before Tahrir, and then there was life in Tahrir. There was the life of failure, frustrations, and depression; and then there was the life of success, glory, and pride. For them, a return to the previous life was out of the question, an attachment to the new one quite natural. Even those who had joined the struggle in its final hours found reason to continue the attachment to the mythical square. Many of them would later speak of those eighteen days in mythological terms—poor and rich standing side by side, Christian and Muslim, men and women, no hatreds or differences, millions of Egyptians, all united by love of country. Soon the square became Egypt, and they became the revolution.

The Egypt of their imagination was a simple one. Egypt was a rich country, yet its people were poor. The reason for their poverty was Mubarak and his corrupt regime. Once corruption was ended, and in the world they constructed, corruption could magically end, Egypt would become prosperous. Legends about Mubarak's wealth were proclaimed. The man had stolen anywhere from $70 billion, as the *Guardian* falsely claimed, to $5 trillion, according to a fabricated quote attributed to Catherine Ashton by *Rose al-Yusuf*. That money, once returned, would transform Egypt. Clever thieves fooled many a man in poor neighborhoods into paying a small amount of money to buy an application for his share in Mubarak's treasures.

Everything that had happened in the past thirty years under Mubarak was pure evil. Burke had captured the exact sentiment two centuries earlier: "To hear some men speak of the late monarchy of France, you would imagine that they were talking of Persia bleeding under the ferocious sword of Taehmas Kouli Khan; or at least describing the barbarous anarchic despotism of Turkey, where the finest countries in the most genial climates in the world are wasted by peace more than any countries have been worried by war; where arts are unknown, where manufactures languish, where science is extinguished, where agriculture decays, where the human race itself melts away and perishes under the eye of the observer."[13] Moreover, everything that was evil was of Mubarak's doing. The Alexandria church bombing? It was Mubarak's security that carried the attack. Sectarianism in Egypt? Mubarak. Insufficient production of wheat? Mubarak. Sexual harassment? The list was endless.

13. Edmund Burke, *Reflections on the Revolution in France.*

The Muslim Brotherhood was viewed as square comrades. There was no need to fear them. Revolutionary Socialists had for years adopted British Trotskyite Chris Harman's words: "On some issues we will find ourselves on the same side as the Islamists against imperialism and the state. This was true, for instance, in many countries during the second Gulf War. It should be true in countries like France or Britain when it comes to combating racism. Where the Islamists are in opposition, our rule should be, with the Islamists sometimes, with the state never."[14] Soon nearly everyone was practicing that slogan. The Brotherhood was merely a scarecrow that Mubarak used. What united us is larger than what divides us, it was proclaimed. Millions were united in toppling Mubarak and would continue to achieve the revolution's goals.

Reality was, of course, quite different. There were never the imagined millions in Tahrir Square in the first place. The square with all its surrounding streets could barely hold 400,000

---

14. Chris Harman, *The Prophet and the Proletariat*.

to begin with. Most of the country had not participated in the revolution; they watched the events on TV and had little attachment to the fairy tale. While the revolutionaries would later lament their fate arguing that their greatest mistake was leaving the square, as Harvard political scientist Tarek Masoud observed, the truth was strikingly different: "You didn't leave the Square. The rest of the country did." Few Egyptians were saddened by Mubarak's resignation. For most Egyptians, however, the revolution had achieved its demand. Mubarak had resigned, and now we can all go back to finding food for our families. The economy was in trouble, tourists had disappeared, and the security situation was frightening. The military certainly agreed with that. For the revolutionaries, however, the revolution was not an event. It was a journey, and soon, one without any identified destination.

Less than forty-eight hours after Mubarak's resignation a new million-man demonstration was announced, scheduled for February 18, to celebrate victory and continue the revolution until it achieves all of its demands. Those demands were ever-growing. Some were at least clear: oust

Ahmed Shafik's government, arrest Mubarak and former regime figures, end the state of emergency, and fire the attorney general. Others were nothing more than slogans: social justice, an end to corruption, or independence of the judiciary. One Friday to the next, the demonstrations never stopped. For many it was one continuous demonstration in Tahrir, which became their camp as well as their home. In later months, returning to the square became akin to recharging their hope and adrenaline. For a while their methods seemed to be working, as every week brought new development, more arrests of former Mubarak ministers, or news of the government resigning. Beneath the surface, the revolutionaries' isolation from the rest of the country was growing.

While the rest of the country was searching for a return to normalcy, normalcy was the last thing the revolutionaries wanted. Change was no longer the goal; the revolution itself became the goal. A Trotskyite motto, the permanent revolution, became theirs. The list of individuals and institutions that belonged to the old order and thus in need of purging continued to grow.

The "remnants of the old regime" became an all-encompassing designation. Everyone had a place on the list: the bureaucracy, judiciary, police, military, religious institutions, anyone who belonged to the previous ruling party, the media, businessmen. Little did the revolutionaries ponder the wisdom of their actions; little did they contemplate the hostility that would result. "It is with them a war or a revolution, or it is nothing,"[15] as Burke remarked. Authority as a concept became scorned. The revolution became a revolution against everything old: tradition, respect, even decency. With their language becoming more and more abusive and their graffiti more vulgar, the revolutionaries' words soon turned into action. Violence would only be a matter of time.

Football ultras led the way. Hardly the typical football fans or even hooligans, they resembled fascist youth movements in their organization and glorification of violence, albeit with a culture that viewed the concept of authority as evil. "All Cops Are Bastards," their banners pro-

---

15. Edmund Burke, *Reflections on the Revolution in France.*

claimed. For the revolutionaries, who could never compete with the Muslim Brotherhood in either numbers or organization, the ultras became their heroes, their violence condoned, their songs to the police becoming theirs:

> We have not forgotten
> Tahrir O Sons of Dirty Women[16]
> The revolution for you was a defeat
> Whom should we go and tell . . .
> Our officers are pimps
> You took a beating that you had not taken for years

The revolution had not been peaceful in the first place, but the cycle was deteriorating by the day. Molotov cocktails thrown at police stations became the most natural act of nonviolence, peeing on the walls of the Interior Ministry the ultimate act of revolutionary zeal. Anarchism had become a lifestyle. Demonstrations became street battles, most often with the police, but sometimes with disgruntled citizens who were fed up with the endless protests taking place in their neighborhoods. Street battles were no

---

16. A song by Zamalek Ultras, also known as Ultras White Knights.

longer fought for goals, after they began no one was quite sure how it had started in the first place, instead they were fought for territory, for possession of streets, for feet, yards, and inches. It was no surprise that mob violence in the UK would be viewed with delight or that Occupy Wall Street would receive the revolutionaries' support, as little differentiated them. It became common for the revolutionaries to publicize the home addresses of those they hated on social media, thereby endorsing mob action against them. There had been torture in Tahrir during the revolution. Those suspected of being thugs or secret police were held and beaten. A confinement tent for suspected thugs became a common sight at the center of the revolutionary camp in Tahrir.

The contradictions were glaring. The revolutionaries who claimed the mantle of human rights were practicing torture. Men who called for the rule of law came to think of themselves as above the law. People who argued for the freedom of the press demanded the silencing of all who criticized them. Champions of democracy rejected people's choices and proclaimed revolutionary legitimacy. Those who stood against military trials were calling for revolutionary trials for their opponents. They had no patience for justice. Instead revolutionary justice became the motto. Maximilien de Robespierre's words were being echoed: "Hence Louis cannot be judged; he is judged already. He is condemned, or the Republic is not absolved. To propose a trial for Louis XVI in any way whatever is to retrograde toward royal and constitutional despotism; it is a counter-revolutionary idea, for it is putting the revolution itself on trial."[17] For them, if the goal were noble, any means was justifiable. As Leon Trotsky wrote: "As for us, we were never concerned with the Kantian-priestly and vegetarian-Quaker prattle about the 'sacredness of human life.' We were revolutionaries in opposition, and have remained revolutionaries in power. To make the individual sacred we must destroy the social order which crucifies him. And this problem can only be solved by blood and iron."[18]

---

17. Robespierre, *Against Granting the King a Trial*.

18. Leon Trotsky, *Terrorism and Communism: A Reply to Karl Kautsky*.

"To make a government requires no great prudence.
Settle the seat of power; teach obedience: and the
work is done. To give freedom is still more easy.
It is not necessary to guide; it only requires to let
go the rein. But to form a *free government;* that is,
to temper together these opposite elements of liberty
and restraint in one consistent work, requires much
thought, deep reflection, a sagacious, powerful, and
combining mind."

(EDMUND BURKE: *Reflections on the Revolution in France*)

A Leader Is Wanted[19]

A Leader is wanted for a people that have always
    been great
A leader is wanted who will protect rights / be just
    between people like Omar Ibn El Khattab
His hearing good so he can listen to the beat
    of our hearts
And his place is between us he should never live
    in palaces
In short . . . a macho man is wanted

"But when the leaders choose to make themselves
bidders at an auction of popularity, their talents, in
the construction of the state, will be of no service.
They will become flatterers instead of legislators;
the instruments, not the guides of the people.
If any of them should happen to propose a scheme
of liberty, soberly limited, and defined with proper

---

19. A song by the band Cairokee.

qualifications, he will be immediately outbid by his competitors, who will produce something more splendidly popular. Suspicions will be raised of his fidelity to his cause. Moderation will be stigmatized as the virtue of cowards; and compromise as the prudence of traitors."

(EDMUND BURKE: *Reflections on the Revolution in France*)

EGYPT COULD NOT BE EXPECTED to wait in limbo until the revolutionaries finished their vendetta against the state. The revolution had unleashed forces long contained and suppressed by Mubarak's authoritarian grip on power. With the repressive hand removed, Pandora's box was suddenly opened. Workers were demanding higher wages, Copts an end to their discrimination, Islamists an Islamic state, women equality, retirees higher benefits. The demands were endless. Even police officers were striking for better pay. The revolution had unleashed a colossal euphoria of expectations, and delivery on all fronts was eagerly awaited.

Upon assuming power, the military had promised a swift transition to democracy and power transfer in six months. The process of amending the Constitution had been initiated by

Mubarak in his last days in power, but it was now more urgent than ever. Who would write the Constitution became the first battle that split those who had united in toppling Mubarak. The Muslim Brotherhood, the best organized and most popular movement in the country, was naturally in favor of a fast-track transition. Non-Islamists on the other hand, were frightened. A swift transition would mean a Brotherhood victory. They needed more time to organize. Like the Brotherhood and other Islamists, the military favored a yes vote. The March 19 referendum became a test of size and appeal. One week before the vote, ElBaradei was sufficiently frightened and asked, in a tweet, the military to cancel the vote, citing Egypt's national interests. Results weren't even close. A whopping 77 percent of the electorate voted against non-Islamists.

The results never sank in. In a repeated phenomenon, whenever they were faced with failure and disasters, non-Islamists would join their revolutionary brethren in blaming anyone but themselves. All actions and events were attributed to an omnipotent SCAF and its devilish schemes, a SCAF that existed only in their imagination. Conspiracy theories, a signature of Egyptian politics, were an easier scapegoat than taking responsibility for one's actions, chasing ghosts simpler than examining root causes. Myths were never challenged. Mubarak, they believed, had allowed the Islamists to grow. In reality, as Tarek Masoud wrote: "If the movement had a head start over liberals, it is not because it had an easier time under Mubarak, but rather—as Brotherhood members are likely to aver—because they have worked harder. No delay in elections will change that."[20] The revolutionaries and the larger non-Islamist camp were growing more isolated from the rest of the country.

Isolation gave birth to delusions, and when delusions ultimately met reality, they either grew more delusional or developed into bitterness and disdain. The initial revolutionary assumption was that the country was united behind their demands and that the few who weren't were "remnants of the old regime," evil people

---

20. Tarek Masoud, "Liberty, Democracy and Discord in Egypt," *The Washingtonian Quarterly* (Fall 2001): 117–129.

who conspired against the people. As the months went by and it became obvious that the majority of Egyptians did not share the revolutionaries' euphoria, the condescension began. Burke had described their likes two centuries earlier: "You will smile here at the consistency of those democratists, who, when they are not on their guard, treat the humbler part of the community with the greatest contempt, whilst, at the same time, they pretend to make them the depositories of all power."[21] Instead of being a heroic people, Egyptians were now called "a slave people" used to submission to the extent of developing Stockholm syndrome, who didn't deserve the revolutionaries' sacrifices. People who were unfamiliar with who Benjamin Franklin was were now quoting him: "Those who would give up essential liberty, to purchase a little temporary safety, deserve neither liberty nor safety." Though, the quote was often falsely attributed to Thomas Jefferson. The older generation was mocked and insulted, the younger one glorified and hallowed. In the following months, every non-

---

21. Edmund Burke, *Reflections on the Revolution in France*.

Islamist demonstration in Tahrir would end up with the same demand among many: the military should hand over power to a presidential council. People's votes were to be ignored and power given to them.

Soon a Jacobin discourse dominated the revolutionaries' worldview. Anyone who did not share their quest for the continuous revolution was a traitor and thus not a true revolutionary. Even old comrades of the square who advocated caution and compromise were showered with contempt. "When they have rendered that deposed power sufficiently black, they then proceed in argument, as if all those who disapprove of their new abuses, must of course be partisans of the old; that those who reprobate their crude and violent schemes of liberty ought to be treated as advocates for servitude."[22] Politicians were frightened. If they dared suggest that perhaps it was time to put an end to the demonstrations game and start playing politics, they were putting themselves at risk of being painted as enemies of the revolution. Burke had remarked

---

22. Edmund Burke, *Reflections on the Revolution in France.*

that: "Men have been sometimes led by degrees, sometimes hurried into things, the whole of which, if they could have seen together, they never would have permitted the most remote approach."[23] Even the few who recognized the disastrous course of action that was being taken found themselves forced to toe the line. Pessimism was treason, the revolutionaries proclaimed, and few dared to object. Speaking of their Western supporters, but truer still of them, Walter Laqueur had written: "The same seems to apply today—better to be mistaken in the right company than be prematurely right in the wrong company. This is the Paris syndrome of a few decades ago—better to be wrong with Sartre than right with Raymond Aron."[24]

Politics was not only a game the revolutionaries refused to play; it was also one they completely disdained. Looking back, that was hardly surprising. The cause of their success in toppling Mubarak was the reason for their failure there-

---

23. Edmund Burke, *Reflections on the Revolution in France.*

24. Walter Laqueur, "The Perils of Wishful Thinking: On Europe and the Middle East, *World Affairs Journal* (March/April 2012).

after. The appeal to abstract principles and empty slogans was instrumental in uniting people against a dictator but was meaningless as a program of elections and governance; the training on the latest technology was ill-suited for developing policy programs; the mobilization outside parties was necessary for a revolution but incapable of winning elections. Faced with an economic crisis, the revolutionaries seemed to think that money grew on trees. Asked to deal with Egypt's endemic problems, the revolutionary representatives suggested seriously that Egypt should collect Suez Canal fees in Egyptian pounds. Offered an opportunity to discuss the country's future with the new finance minister on a TV program, they boldly proposed growing wheat on the roofs of buildings to solve Egypt's wheat shortage. Complicated questions of economics and governance were not for them. The street was where the glory was, politics a boring process. Burke had called our attention to the fact that for them: "A cheap, bloodless reformation, a guiltless liberty, appear flat and vapid to their taste. There must be a great change of scene; there must be a magnificent stage effect; there must be a grand spectacle to rouse the imagination."[25]

The generation that had left politics for human rights advocacy could not be suddenly expected to make the transition back. Human rights defenders are fighting for a noble cause. They do not negotiate, they never compromise. There is no negotiation between the abused and the abuser, no compromise between the tortured and the torturer. As Burke wrote: "They have 'the rights of men.' Against these there can be no prescription; against these no agreement is binding: these admit no temperament, and no compromise: any thing withheld from their full demand is so much of fraud and injustice."[26] Pragmatism is not a virtue in the world of human rights advocacy. Asked what he had in mind for his movement's future, April 6 founder Ahmed Maher replied: "April 6 will monitor Parliament's performance and confront any mistakes. . . . The group will continue to mobilize in Tahrir Square

25. Edmund Burke, *Reflections on the Revolution in France*.
26. Edmund Burke, *Reflections on the Revolution in France*.

when necessary."[27] His colleague in the movement, Mohamed Adel described their priorities: "building a new state, societal reform, and putting pressure on anyone in power."[28] If they clung to their previous practices, it was because they knew no other.

The contempt the revolutionaries held for politics was most apparent in their accusations against the Muslim Brotherhood. Its greatest crime, in their eyes, was having betrayed the demands of the revolution and cutting a deal with SCAF. Regardless of the truthfulness of the accusation, that it was viewed as an accusation in the first place is remarkable. Politics by its very nature is the art of negotiation, compromise, and cutting deals. No political actor is likely to achieve all his aspirations, at least not one who does not have a monopoly on the state. Given that the revolutionaries had the weakest hand among the three contending groups, they should have been the one who most sought a

27. Sarah Carr, "6 April: Genealogy of a Youth Movement," *Jadaliyya*, April 5, 2012.

28. Sarah Carr, "6 April: Genealogy of a Youth Movement," *Jadaliyya*, April 5, 2012.

deal. Nothing of the sort took place. The few non-Islamists who were willing to negotiate with SCAF and guarantee a state where Islamists would not dominate the country and transform society in return for preserving the military's interests were pronounced traitors by the revolutionaries. Negotiations were a betrayal to the blood of martyrs, they said. In the end it was all or nothing. Naturally, they got nothing.

The revolutionaries' worst offense, however, was their complete ignorance of the country they sought to transform. Their imaginary Egypt had no relationship to the actual Egypt. When Salafis began demanding an Islamic state, many a revolutionary expressed surprise and admitted not knowing Salafis existed in Egypt. When attacks on Christians intensified, many a revolutionary were astonished by the level of sectarianism in the country. When Egyptians elected Islamists to Parliament, the revolutionaries could not understand why they didn't vote for the revolution's party. When Mohamed Morsi and Ahmed Shafik received the highest number of votes in the first round of the presidential election, there was genuine shock among the revolutionaries. Burke had described their French ancestors as "men who never had seen the state so much as in a picture."[29] His words have never rang truer.

⁓

> "But what is liberty without wisdom, and without virtue? It is the greatest of all possible evils; for it is folly, vice, and madness, without tuition or restraint. Those who know what virtuous liberty is, cannot bear to see it disgraced by incapable heads, on account of their having high-sounding words in their mouths. Grand, swelling sentiments of liberty, I am sure I do not despise. They warm the heart; they enlarge and liberalize our minds; they animate our courage in a time of conflict."
>
> (EDMUND BURKE: *Reflections on the Revolution in France*)

> "In the weakness of one kind of authority, and in the fluctuation of all, the officers of an army will remain for some time mutinous and full of faction, until some popular general, who understands the art of conciliating the soldiery, and who possesses the true spirit of command, shall draw the eyes of all men upon himself. Armies will obey him on his personal

---

29. Edmund Burke, *Reflections on the Revolution in France*.

account. There is no other way of securing military obedience in this state of things. But the moment in which that event shall happen, the person who really commands the army is your master; the master (that is little) of your king, the master of your assembly, the master of your whole republic."

(EDMUND BURKE: *Reflections on the Revolution in France*)

DURING THE MAGICAL EIGHTEEN DAYS of Tahrir Square, and while the revolution was still in its honeymoon, Amr Bargisi, one of Egypt's most astute observers, said: "Egypt lacks the sort of political culture that can sustain a liberal democracy."[30] The reason for his pessimism was not that he thought Egyptians are inferior to other peoples or that Egypt "seems to lack even the basic mental ingredients,"[31] as David Brooks wrote.

His pessimism was grounded in a simple fact of life. You cannot achieve a result if there is no

---

30. Amr Bargisi, "Where Should Egypt Go From Here?: Egypt Doesn't Have a Democratic Culture," *Wall Street Journal,* February 2, 2011.

31. David Brooks, "Defending the Coup," *New York Times,* July 4, 2013.

one trying to achieve it. A liberal democracy is not born out of thin air. It requires the existence of liberal democrats. And if the term means something more than people who are simply not Islamists and not extreme leftists, then they are absent in Egyptian politics. There are very few liberals in Egypt, not because Egyptians are averse to liberalism or are different from any other people, but because there is no liberalism in Egypt. There is no liberal discourse in the public square. People cannot belong to an ideology that does not exist. With hardly any liberal books written in Arabic and no translations of the major works of Western liberalism, those liberals in Egypt are but a privileged few who are able and willing to read in a foreign language.

Today, Egypt's former revolutionaries are split between the submissive and the delusional, between those who have become no more than cheerleaders for a military coup and those who continue to dream of an endless revolution—or, as Leszek Kolakowski once remarked, "between lovers of prostitutes and lovers of clouds: those who know only the satisfaction of the moment . . . and those who lose themselves in otiose imaginings."[32] It is easy to mistake them for helpless victims, men caught like Oedipus in a tragedy they cannot control. Greek tragedies, however, have little to offer in understanding the story of the Egyptian revolution and its failure, but perhaps another Greek contribution to civilization might be better suited for the task— Greek mythology. Unless they begin to learn from their mistakes, unless they embark on a journey of discovering their own country, unless they educate themselves not on the newest technology but on the oldest books, unless they start offering their countrymen something more than abstract principles, they are forever doomed, like Sisyphus, condemned eternally to repeatedly roll a heavy rock up a hill only to have it roll down again as it nears the top. An eternity of fruitless labor and endless disappointment.

---

32. Leszek Kolakowski, *Modernity on Endless Trial.*

Today, after the revolution and its hopes and disappointments, Egypt finds itself in a world it knows all too well —faith in the deliverance offered by one man. The hope is now invested in a military commander, Abdel Fattah el-Sisi. It is dictatorship by demand, as it were. The country has been here before. For two decades, from 1954 to 1970, Gamal Abdel Nasser gave Egypt its moment of enthusiasm and then led it to defeat and heartbreak. It would take a leap of faith, and luck beyond what history offers, to believe that this faith in a redeemer will yield a better harvest than the one before it.

Throughout the previous three years and during the turmoil that shook Egypt to its core, I was in endless conversation with a small group of Egyptian liberals who cared deeply for their country. The three years would not have been the same without them; this article would not have been the same without their endless comments and opinions throughout that period. I am forever indebted to them.

ABOUT THE AUTHOR

SAMUEL TADROS is a senior fellow at the Hudson Institute's Center for Religious Freedom and a contributor to the Hoover Institution's Herbert and Jane Dwight Working Group on Islamism and the International Order. His most recent book is *Motherland Lost: The Egyptian and Coptic Quest for Modernity* (Hoover Institution Press, 2013).

Born and raised in Egypt, he received his M.A. in Democracy and Governance from Georgetown University and his B.A. in Political Science from the American University in Cairo. He has studied at the Coptic Theological Seminary in Cairo.

HERBERT AND JANE DWIGHT
WORKING GROUP ON
ISLAMISM AND THE
INTERNATIONAL ORDER

THE HERBERT AND JANE DWIGHT WORKING
GROUP ON ISLAMISM AND THE INTERNATIONAL
ORDER seeks to engage in the task of reversing Islamic radicalism through reforming and strengthening the legitimate role of the state across the entire Muslim world. Efforts will draw on the intellectual resources of an array of scholars and practitioners from within the United States and abroad, to foster the pursuit of modernity, human flourishing, and the rule of law and reason in Islamic lands—developments that are critical to the very order of the international system.

The Working Group is cochaired by Hoover fellows Fouad Ajami and Charles Hill, with an active participation by Hoover Institution Director John Raisian. Current core membership includes Russell A. Berman and Abbas Milani, with contributions from Zeyno Baran, Marius Deeb, Reuel Marc Gerecht, Ziad Haider, R. John Hughes, Nibras Kazimi, Bernard Lewis, Habib C. Malik, Camille Pecastaing, Itamar Rabinovich, Lieutenant Colonel Joel Rayburn, Lee Smith, Samuel Tadros, Joshua Teitelbaum, and Tunku Varadarajan.

Freedom or Terror: Europe Faces Jihad
Russell A. Berman

*The Myth of the Great Satan:
A New Look at America's Relations with Iran*
Abbas Milani

Torn Country: Turkey between Secularism and Islamism
Zeyno Baran

Islamic Extremism and the War of Ideas: Lessons from Indonesia
R. John Hughes

The End of Modern History in the Middle East
Bernard Lewis

The Wave: Man, God, and the Ballot Box in the Middle East
Reuel Marc Gerecht

Trial of a Thousand Years: World Order and Islamism
Charles Hill

Jihad in the Arabian Sea
Camille Pecastaing

The Syrian Rebellion
Fouad Ajami

Motherland Lost: The Egyptian and Coptic Quest for Modernity
Samuel Tadros

Iraq after America: Strongmen, Sectarians, Resistance
Joel Rayburn

[For a list of essays published under the auspices of the
WORKING GROUP ON ISLAMISM AND THE INTERNATIONAL ORDER,
please see page ii.]

INDEX